Wedding Cake

A Woman's Recipe for Fulfillment

Ann Ross

ISBN: 978-0692570821
Heiress Ross Multimedia Group, LLC)
ISBN: 0692570829

Disclaimer

The author makes no guarantees with respect to the results or effectiveness of the suggested exercises. This book is sold with the understanding that the author is not engaged in rendering any professional services or advice. The ideas offered in this publication are based on the author's experience and have been effective for her. The author shall not be held liable for any loss or damages incurred as a consequence, directly or indirectly, from the use of the information in this publication.

Dedication

I'm dedicating this book to all the Queens in my life, especially my mother who taught me what a strong courageous woman should be. A true Proverbs 31 woman, she taught me how to stand by being an example. Thank you Mom!

Contents

Acknowledgments

I wish to express my sincerest gratitude to those who supported me on this journey whether through time, encouragement, wisdom, or knowledge.

To my editor, Andrea Glass: from the first time we spoke I knew that you were the one to assist me in bringing this project alive. Thank you for understanding and capturing the true essence of my thoughts and knowing the power of the words that would be read. Thank you for your guidance and support knowing I was a first time writer, and the care you have shown me through this process. Your work is amazing and the world is better for the talented gift you have within that you graciously share.

To my designer, Nick Scribner: you are a super rock star, and I'm grateful for the day my brother gave me your contact information. Never in a million years could I have imaged that I would experience the greatness of your talent. Thank you for always making yourself available to me, no matter day or night. For all the calls and emails you accepted of my changes, and whatever I asked you to do you willingly made it happen. Thank you and know more great things are ahead.

To Jasmine Brand: thank you for taking the time to encourage and inspire me to be greater. Your words are used to empower many, and your testimony of greatness and success lead me to believe with hard work and dedication I too could succeed. *"Many have great ideas, but it's the ones who execute that have the success."* (www.theJasmineBrand.com)

To my Pastor, Byron Ravenell: you are a humble prayer warrior, a true servant of the most High God, and I'm forever grateful to you and your family. It's your prayers and words of encouragement that kept me going through this journey. For that I'm eternally grateful!

To my Auntie Angie: you're a booming cymbal that has the ability to gain the attention of those you're seeking to hear the sound. Without that boom this book would not have been birthed. It was you who encouraged me to write, not knowing what I would write or what it would produce. But your belief in me was greatness. For that I thank you.

To my Mom: this book is dedicated to you. You were the first example of greatness and strength I had known. Through struggle and challenge you raised three children on your own and managed to maintain your beauty—outer and inner—the true essence of a virtuous woman. Thank you for all the hard, true, loving, encouraging, and supportive conversations and deeds. No one on earth is greater than you!

To my children: thank you for being everything that Mom needed through this process—understanding, loving, encouraging, and supportive. Know that you both are my hearts joy, and I'm grateful that God chose me to be your mom. Thank you for being proud of me, and know this is all for you both. Legacy!

Finally, but always first in my heart and mind as I was always first in your mind, thought, and purpose, to the God I serve. Mere words can't express my gratitude for the wisdom and knowledge you've granted to me to share with the world. Through my process I've been allowed to see that you're always with me, through the goods times and the challenges of life. Without you I never could have completed this book; however, you reminded me to tap into the inner strength which is where you dwell. To you God, I'm eternally grateful and can only give back a surrendered life as your servant.

Introduction
(My Journey)

All my life I'd been looking for love and the fulfillment of a dream of having a husband who would love me completely and unconditionally. I searched for love in relationship after relationship, yet none seemed to satisfy me wholly. Many heartbreaks later, I figured something was wrong with me, so I eventually stopped interacting and went into isolation, which allowed depression to set in.

I had gotten so caught up in the dream of marriage and what religion dictated about it, that every man I came across was "The One" without knowing his characteristics—or whether he was a bad boy, crazy, abusive, or a loving man. My constant words because I was so religious were: "God told me he was the one" (lies I told myself). Many women, whether religious or not, and because of desperation, create the illusion of "He Must Be the One" with whomever says, "I love you."

I'm reminded of one relationship in particular where I convinced myself into believing this one was the one. At the time I was going through a financial challenge and was homeless with a child, and here came this man saying all the right things. Now, because of his seeming kindness, I convinced myself that yes, he wanted me and he was the one. So when he told me to move in, of course I ran to him. Once I did, I began my unmarried wifely duties. I know it sounds like an oxymoron doesn't it: an unmarried wife. This term meant I cooked, cleaned, paid his bills and mine, and yes, even performed bedroom duties, activities a typical wife would do. However, I had no commitment from him, let alone a marriage certificate. For three years I acted as the unmarried wife, and one day I decided to consult with God in my time of prayer, something I had failed to do prior to getting involved in this relationship. In prayer, it became clear to me that I could marry this man (not that he asked). Yet, I also felt God's intention for my life was a greater purpose full of blessings that were not intended for this man.

I knew that if I married him I would be married (Yay!), but in exchange for marriage my purpose, destiny, and blessings would be neglected. Many would think that's a lot to forfeit—one's purpose, destiny, and blessings. However, because of my strong desire for marriage and because I felt empty in many areas of my life I thought he would fill, I decided purpose and destiny weren't more important than this relationship, so I stayed.

Then it happened. The man I was willing to forfeit everything for told me he heard from God through another woman that he should end our relationship. It's amazing to me how people use God to make their decision seem valid or righteous, like I did in the beginning.

Through my heartbreak, I became hard and bitter and built a brick wall, because someone I was willing to forfeit everything for wasn't willing to do the same for me. I learned that as women we're generally weaker emotionally, so we must be careful not to give our valuables— our love, heart, emotions, thoughts, purpose, and destiny—to those who aren't worthy. So here I was brokenhearted again over a relationship that wouldn't produce the blessings in my life.

Many women have no clue what we're really forfeiting when we get into nonproductive relationships. We sacrifice the ability to produce fruit: loving relationships, business ideas, projects, etc. If you look at every fruit, it contains seeds which produce more fruit, and in most there are multiple seeds in one piece of fruit. As women, we have good seeds in our lives that will open the door for more opportunities, such as creative ideas, inventions, etc. Yet when stagnated by unproductive relationships, we're sidetracked because we wonder how to fix the relationship or why it's happening to us.

I spent a year getting over this relationship and releasing the "why is this happening to me?" attitude, although I know I had allowed it. In my brokenness, I sought out God and prayed fervently, because I needed to know what I could do to make sure this didn't happen again, and I wanted to know how to be "whole" in every area of my life so I didn't need another person so desperately.

I've always been interested in learning, and I enjoy studying new ideas, which was helpful in my initial process of becoming whole. I was prompted to read and study the Bible, and the stories I was drawn to were the Books of Ruth and Esther. In my studies, I discovered these were women of character, full of love, gratitude, humility, kindness, and longevity. Women who instead of trusting their thoughts and beliefs relied on more than their own thoughts and sought wise counsel to help them get to the next level in their pursuit of purpose and destiny.

One of the passages I liked in the Book of Ruth was: "Blessed are you of the Lord, my daughter! For you have shown more kindness at the end than at the beginning...And now, my daughter do not fear, I will do for you all that you request, for all the people of my town will know that you are a virtuous woman."

Now when I first read this, I got excited, although I knew I hadn't been a virtuous woman. As an avid Bible reader, I knew that in Proverbs, a book of wisdom describes the attributes of a Virtuous Woman: the ability to live and love in **Faith**, she desires God's will for her life and follows His ways. As a **Wife** she is a helper to her husband, is trustworthy, respects him, and does him good all her life. As a **Mother**, she teaches her children the ways of righteousness and God, she nurtures and disciplines them with care, is concerned with her and her family's **Health**, and prepares healthy food for them. As a woman of **Business,** she knows how to budget her **Finances.** And she's a woman of **Beauty**, and more.

I figured the best way to be a virtuous woman was to connect with those I thought were virtuous, because of the saying "Birds of a feather flock together." However, it's wise to be careful, as those we think are in the same category may have an outside appearance of what they should look like, while in their hearts they're far from the complete package.

I was met with plenty of negativity on my journey to wholeness, yet I was determined to know how to be a virtuous woman and to be a complete, fulfilled person in my thoughts and emotions. As I continued my studies, I read the Book of Esther, where I learned about favor and the preparation it took for ordinary women, deemed unfit or unqualified, to become a Queen.

While I desired to have better results in my life, I knew I first needed to do things differently than I did in the past. So in prayer I asked God to teach me how to be a better me, and to make me whole so I would be self-reliant and self-loving rather than relying on attention and love from others.

Honestly thought, when I began my process of becoming whole, my goal was to be a better me in order to be ready for marriage. I figured it would lead me to my husband. However, what I found was this process led me to myself. It helped me understand that without making myself a priority in my life, I couldn't be of any value to anyone else. This didn't mean I would have it all together, but it meant that rather than allowing others to be of more importance in my life, I was choosing to make myself the front runner.

Many people might call my actions selfish, yet I understood that choosing me first was allowing me to be there for others. Had I not taken this time to grow, I would not have been able to write this book, or advise women, or encourage others to be all they desire to be. I learned through my process of coming to wholeness that although everyone is unique in certain areas, we have similarities that make us relatable to each other. Regardless of one's culture, age, or preferences, every woman has challenges in relationships, self-esteem, self-worth, finances, business, discovering purpose, and more. And if we have related issues and challenges, then there must be a formula for change—and ultimately fulfillment.

My journey was a 14-year process of bumps and bruises. You must appreciate that before a product can be presented to the public, it has to be tried and tested for effectiveness. I can truly say that I've been tried and tested in this process as an employee, wife, single mom, minister, friend, entrepreneur, and advisor. Those tests and trials have brought me to the understanding that I'm a beautiful, gifted, loving, kind, talented, creative, unstoppable, unshakeable woman who has attained a strong foundation of self-worth.

My life isn't perfect by any means, and I still have challenges; however, the difference between before and after my journey is I've learned to implement specific tools to refocus and get back to my position of wholeness. This process has taught me that although I'm not perfect, the ideal of perfection keeps me striving forward, which drives me to excellence.

So many women live their lives to be married, and I too was one who desired that one true love. I thought this journey to self-worth would help me become a better me for a man. As I discovered more about myself and what I truly desired and aspired to become, I realized I was enough, with or without a man. Most of us do so much to make ourselves more appealing to a man, but rarely do we take the time or opportunity to do as much for ourselves.

Our desire for marriage motivates us to lose weight and to change our style of dress, makeup, and hair. We're constantly looking at the outer appearance to provide an illusion of completeness, when what needs growth is our inner being. This fantasy of completeness through the outer appearance attempts to provide a reflection of the inner, but it lacks the substance wholeness provides. This is why when some women get in relationships, men become disinterested, because the person who had the appearance of completeness on the outer was incomplete on the inner. We haven't taken the opportunity to deal with our inner being, since we're so focused on pleasing with the outer appearance. And just maybe no one's given us the guidance before!

Over the years, I've spoken with many married couples who've been together for decades, and the consistency of most men's conversation about their wives is that although it was her outer appearance that attracted him, it was her inner beauty that sustained him. This is what assisted these couples in maintaining a healthy marriage. Understand ladies that when you're complete within, low self-worth and lack of confidence disappear.

Know that regardless of your decision whether to be whole or live a life full of illusions, your relationships and outcomes will be determined by you, and only you have the power to change. The power that fulfillment provides is the ability to know who you are and what you want, which creates a criteria for any relationship that's to be developed in your life. Whether a working relationship, friendship, family relationship, or intimate relationship, when you know who you are, you're able to properly access what you want and what God wants for you.

The process begins with a vision of your life and what the complete you looks like. Then the plan comes into place on how to become whole, and it begins with addressing who you are now and what areas need work in order to be who you strive to be. What you'll discover is once you've arrived at fulfillment, you'll attract like-minded individuals who have been on the same path.

Why Wedding Cake?

During the wedding cake portion of the marriage reception, the couple has the opportunity to share something special about each other. In any relationship either you'll share your complete self, which will be a benefit to both you and your mate, or you'll share a life of emptiness and illusion.

In my time of preparing for marriage, I can remember my mother speaking to me about a hope chest. (Hope Chest/Dowry Chest: used to collect items such as clothing, house linens, and valuables by an unmarried woman in anticipation of married life.) Part of the process of collecting the items of an unmarried woman was to use her own needlework (art of sewing/embroidery) skills to construct a trousseau (clothes, household linen, and other belongings collected by a bride for her marriage). This process was time-consuming work and the equivalent of planning and saving for marriage.

When my mother explained the practice, she stated that this was done in her era for women who were praying to God for a husband. And based on the woman's faith, she would put certain items in a chest for her wedding day. Women today still believe in and hope for their opportunity at love and marriage. However, many may not understand that just as in times of old in the preparation of the hope chest—putting away/storing valuables—it's necessary to prepare mentally, spiritually, emotionally, and physically for a successful marriage and life. Becoming complete will do more than prepare you for marriage; it will enable you to prepare for business and family, and to be a more effective individual in every area of life.

I'm reminded of an image from my childhood of planning my wedding day. Barbie and Ken would get married every other day in my home, with me humming the traditional wedding processional; you know the one you're humming right now: "Dum dum da dum, dum dum da dum."

Yes, I planned my wedding from childhood up until I was 30 years old, until I received a revelation that it was more than a wedding day. I was really planning for a lifelong journey to discover my purpose, to become complete enough to share the wealth of knowledge, love, and encouragement to aid others in achieving fulfillment.

Like most women, we've lived our lives for the white dress, bridesmaids, ceremony, and that amazing moment when we and our groom feed each other wedding cake. We might think the kiss is the most important part of the wedding, but the most fun comes when it's time for wedding cake. That's when we share for the first time as a married couple, something that's tangible and something we must give the other person. It also symbolizes a full task or completeness, as once the wedding cake is cut that's basically the end of the first chapter or page: the wedding.

In making cakes, there's a process: you gather all the ingredients and utensils and prepare the oven for baking. For wedding cakes, the process is similar to baking any cake, yet each wedding cake is unique. Some are single layers and many are multiple layers, which require more ingredients and much more care.

When I was growing up, the most exciting parts of baking a cake were getting the chance to lick the bowl and utensils after the batter was complete and the anticipation of the cake coming out of the oven. The aromas in the house from each process were different but memorable.

One day when my mom was baking, I asked what certain ingredients tasted like, as my assumption was they each must taste good individually, which was why the cake was so good. I probably bugged her too much that day, because her next words were, "Just taste them." So I did. I tasted the flour, which was bland, no taste. I tasted the baking powder, eggs, and oil which were all tasteless. Now when I got to the vanilla, I figured since it smelled so good it was going to be the tastiest, and to my disappointment it wasn't; it too was bland even though it had such an amazing aroma. I think the only tasty ingredients were the brown and white sugars, but even alone they didn't give a complete flavor; they were just sweet.

Typically in most of our lives just like with the cake ingredients, we have one or more area—whether relationships, finances, or career—that may be complete, but because other areas are not, it makes even the complete areas look incomplete. I believe that to get the most out of life, every area must be whole. Not that they'll be perfect, but there's an understanding that wholeness comes from a place of process and work.

You must understand that regardless of where you are economically, spiritually, physically, or geographically, everyone has the ability to become someone greater. It's only with the proper tools, information, and preparation that the outcome promises to be satisfying and full of life-giving changes.

In these next few Chapters I'll share my journey and the recipe I've been given for my Wedding Cake—a complete process toward wholeness. Remember, everyone's wedding cake will be different depending on how many layers and your decorations and flavors, but the basic ingredients are the same. This process—whether baking a wedding cake or journeying toward wholeness—is not just for a relationship with a man. It's more about becoming a woman of integrity, valor, virtue, and honor, which will make you a more effective wife, mother, entrepreneur, employee, and friend—but most of all give you an identity and purpose.

As you move forward, the process may not be easy for you. For some it may be a challenge, yet it will be one of the most rewarding paths you ever take, as the finished product is your wholeness as a woman. This process is necessary, especially for those women who are seeking to be married, as you must understand that without being whole within, there's no one who will complete you. And if you marry for someone else to complete you, you'll be disappointed and frustrated, because the other person can never live up to your needs and expectations.

Only you have what you need, as it was placed in you from the beginning, and only you can bring it out of you. Your fulfillment of every empty space in your life is dependent upon your digging deep within yourself to bring up what will make you whole. To have a successful relationship, remember that half and half doesn't make a whole—only two whole individuals will make a whole relationship.

Whether your goal is wholeness, fulfillment, success, value, identity, self-worth, or transformation (all interchangeable throughout the book), this is the path for you! It's my hope for you that through reading *Wedding Cake*, you'll come into the realization of who you are and not allow any individual or circumstance to define your wholeness or keep you from fulfillment and achieving success.

Let's start the process to Wholeness and Fulfillment!

In order for you to come to fulfillment in your life, take the time to discover your own thoughts in the Note Section of each Chapter.

Notes

_____

_____

_____

_____

_____

_____

_____

_____

_____

_____

_____

_____

_____

_____

_____

_____

_____

_____

_____

_____

_____

_____

Meditation (And Manifestation)

Now, this is probably going to be the hardest thing you'll have to do on your journey. So let's tackle it first! For me, meditation is a time of quieting myself so I can receive instructions. Then I affirm and speak what I heard in order to see the manifestation. So here's the formula: Meditation + Affirmation + Declaration = Manifestation.

In meditation you have to silence your mind so you can focus for a period of time. For many of us that's difficult to do, because even in quiet times, it's tough to focus. We seem to have the chores and necessities of life we're constantly thinking about.

However, meditation helps you get on track to where you want to go, in this case that place is wholeness. So I think it's worth the effort. Part of the meditation/manifestation formula is about concentrating on your topic of wholeness; you need to focus on what wholeness means to you and what it looks like for you. Keep in mind a Wedding Cake—how many layers do you want to your wholeness? What flavors (areas) do you want? What does your cake (wholeness) look like?

In this process you must wake up with these thoughts and go to bed at night with the same center of attention. The formula is not just the thoughts you think but also the words you speak. Ask yourself this: how many times have you contradicted your thoughts with your words, and consequently the outcome you were seeking was a failure? Why did your thoughts or intentions fail? Because your thoughts and spoken words didn't agree.

Here's an example most women can relate to: you *thought* you should lose weight but *spoke* the words that you wanted a donut for breakfast and a burger for lunch. I would have to say that donuts and burgers don't go with losing weight. Do they? So at that moment your thoughts didn't agree with your spoken words. And off you go and get the donut and burger; you gain a couple of pounds and wonder why you can't lose weight. Your thoughts and words must agree in order to meditate and manifest what you want.

One way to focus on your desire is to think of where you were a couple of years ago compared to where you are now. You may discover that you're not the same individual you were three years ago. In that case, you need a transition in your thinking, because you can't base your "now" on a "then" situation. What I mean is you can't properly access where you need to go if you're still in an old mindset.

There was a time when I weighed 265 pounds and wore a size 24 dress. Yes, that was me! I took initiative and did what I needed to do to lose the weight. Yet after the weight loss, my perception of myself was still a size 24. This resulted in my continuing to lose weight after I had already lost over 100 lbs. I continued to wear extra-large clothes, because I hadn't focused my mind or transitioned to the thought that I was no longer a size 24 but now a size 6. It took my Aunt who asked me to go shopping with her, to prompt a new perception of myself. As I began to try on clothes, I saw the transformation, which provided a new outlook on my appearance.

So understand that you can't have success without looking at where you've come from, because you must realize that the person you were yesterday is not the person you are today. And the person you are today is not the person you want to be—so your focus must be on becoming the future you, the whole you.

Meditation creates an atmosphere of serenity, a place you come to where every concern, care, or form of stress ceases to exist. Not that the concern has gone away, but you want to get to a place in your mind that no longer has the space or room to house any negativity as you fill it with thoughts of peace and relaxation.

You need to be determined to get to that place. Why is it that you can't have serenity on the job or in an environment that's not physically conducive, like where chaos is evident? It's because your brain or mental experiences have taught you that your physical condition or state is reality, therefore forcing you to conform to natural realities. Now I'm not saying living in a fantasy world is the key to serenity, but I am saying not to allow your physical condition, circumstances, or chaos around you to dictate your mindset or your thoughts.

There's a scripture I'm reminded of that reads: "Do not be conformed to this world, but be transformed by the renewal of your mind." It's simple to see the understanding of this, because life experiences, situations, and environments have the ability to shape our thoughts and actions. For example, have you ever had the best day, and someone comes along with a bad attitude or negative energy or cuts you off on the road, and that good day you were having shifted into the attitude of that negative individual or situation. That's what's meant by conforming, because instead of standing out and being unique or separate, you become like the environment you're part of.

Let me tell you, it's acceptable to be the oddball or unique individual when it comes to serenity, joy, and happiness. While everyone is stressed, depressed, and struggling you can live a different life. And if those around you aspire to live in serenity, you can share this journey of meditation and wholeness with them. Keep in mind that the place of calm won't occur because you don't have the same issues or circumstances as others; it's just that you're determined to change or renew your mind regarding those same issues or circumstances.

Something I've learned about peace through meditation is that whatever's happening in your reality doesn't last long because of the change that happens in your mind and thoughts. Ever have a thought of someone or felt inclined to call someone on the phone, and in that same instance that person you were thinking of showed up or called you? That occurrence manifests simply by your thoughts and the focus or meditation on that person.

It's with that same focus that your wholeness will be achieved. You must be determined to direct your thoughts on your desired outcome and then watch as things shift toward what you've focused on. That's the place of serenity, a place in your mind where peace and relaxation is produced through focused energy, and in exchange you're uplifted, renewed, and refreshed.

Meditation is not a one-time event or a one-day process. It's a every day practice, and in order to experience the fullness of its results, you must be consistent and not quit no matter what presents itself. Distractions, obstacles, impatience, laziness, and other excuses can sidetrack you from your daily practice. Don't let them! Because once you start to see results manifest, you'll still want to continue a daily practice with the same determination of a focused mind to maintain your favorable outcomes.

You must be single-minded in the pursuit of wholeness. You must not be moved by any circumstance or situation. You must not get sidetracked by life's challenges. The moment you focus on negativity is the moment you become distracted or discouraged and start to focus on illusions and false realities.

In the process of meditation you must be content with where you are in order to focus your mind on wholeness. If you're frustrated with your now, you'll do one of two things: either force the process to escalate the results or give up and quit. Now for the sake of the title of this book, *Wedding Cake,* the one thing I know about baking cake is if you take the cake out of the oven before it's done, the cake will be undercooked and inedible.

Why do I say you must be "content" rather than "comfortable"? Because being content means you're at ease in your mind, but although you're at ease, you're not comfortable in that place. If you were comfortable, it would mean you'd reached a place of sufficiency and therefore had no need to continue. You were already at the place you desired to be.

To start the meditation process, find a quiet place to sit and still your mind. A place where you don't have to be available to anyone else; you don't need to put on a fake smile; you don't need to smell good; you don't need make-up. It's just an atmosphere for being—not doing! For me that place is the bathroom in my home or at the beach (or anywhere near water). During my time of meditation, I isolate myself from anything that's noisy in my life. I know isolation isn't easy for most of us, as being around people is essential. However, for this process, it can be a hindrance to forward movement.

When I first began meditating, there was no social media so that was the least of my worries. But I needed to decrease my time on distractions like the telephone, television, and nights out. Keep in mind, as a mother my options were limited, because I still had an obligation to my children.

So as part of meditation, I would take walks on the beach, or in my neighborhood—whenever I could fit it into my schedule. After I cared for my children at night, I would set aside a separate time for my meditation or quiet time. I would light candles and meditate on every good thing I needed and wanted in my life. I focused on God and inquired of my purpose and destiny and how to be single-minded in my thoughts and goals.

Recipe for Meditation

1) Quiet time.
2) Focus.
3) Determine to remain in the place of serenity.

Exercise

Take a walk on the beach or in your neighborhood, and focus your mind on what you'll look and feel like whole in every area of your life.

During my time of meditation I found that in quietness, I had the opportunity for the Higher Power, or God, to show me my habits and characteristics, good, bad, and ugly. As I saw myself revealed, I was prompted to have a dialogue with God in prayer (similar to meditation only you listen *and* speak).

Something I've noticed as I speak to many women is that most of their prayer time is spent asking God for a husband or for money. However, the true reason for prayer is to receive instruction for what you're desiring. There's a verse that reads "...your Father knows what you need before you ask him." So if God knows what I need before I ask, then why am I asking? This says to me that since He knows what I need, the next thing is to tell me how to get it.

Yet in order to obtain certain results, you have to see yourself already having them. For example, if you're asking God for a million dollars but you have a shopping problem, what's the point of asking for a million dollars if you don't know how to maintain it? But if you took responsibility for the issue of shopping, you would take the necessary steps to correct the matter, and once that's done, you might see yourself with that million dollars and know how to maintain it and make the money work for you.

In order to focus on becoming the whole you, you need to concentrate on what's true about you: your good qualities. Focusing on the truth causes some people pain, because many live a reality of lies and fantasy. How can a lie or fantasy be reality? Because if you've lied to yourself for a long time, your lies become your reality. Maybe you've created some fantasy relationship over the years since childhood (what woman hasn't?). Perhaps the relationship you're in isn't fulfilling because of the illusion you've created in your fantasy, so you're unhappy with the present reality, which is truth.

Truth causes you to face what you'd rather put behind you or bury deep within, but when you bury anything it always comes up again. That's why it's so important to meditate on the truth and for you to know that truth isn't there to harm you. If you live with it and know how to accept truth, it will free your mind, will, and emotions. You create an atmosphere of freedom because you're no longer in fear of someone finding out your truth. You're able to live freely, creating less stress and anxiety, enabling you to be free in your body and soul which produces a healthier, whole you.

It's difficult to know the truth about yourself if you've lived a lie or in fantasy so long that it's hard to believe what you're being shown about you. I'll never forget while driving down the street, a friend and I were talking, and she told me that sometimes you have to be honest with yourself because truth be known, God already knows you, your likes, and dislikes, so why try to create a mask. Many of us live behind a mask in fear that someone will see the real us, which creates a prison, because you always have to be on your best behavior, when the truth is you may not be having a good day, or you like someone but still have to hide behind the mask.

When she made the statement, it was so liberating for me, as the only being of importance I should be concerned with knowing me, already knew me completely. In that moment, I decided since my Higher Power already knew who I was, I was no longer going to live a lie; it was time for me to know the truth about me.

This is where it got deep for me, because now the real meditation began; the process of quieting yourself is preparing you for your truth. If you're bombarded with truth in the beginning just like taking the cake out of the oven too soon, you'll fall off or quit. Discovering the truth is a painful process when you've been living behind a mask for many years, as most of us have.

My truth came when I had to focus on all my past failures in relationships. I discovered in those relationships, I gave up my most valuable possession—my self-respect! I had to come to terms with the fact that although I had given it away, it was my choice and pleasure to give. Why? My self-esteem was so low, I equated love or confidence with a touch or acceptance from a man.

How wrong could I be? While meditating on this fact, I had to be honest with myself and confess that one of my issues was acceptance and knowing true love. Once again, I turned to prayer and my dialogue with God. Now prayer can come through speaking, writing, or reading, but mostly listening! One of the key points of prayer once again is to get instruction on what you're asking for—so you speak and listen.

I've found for many women, we know exactly what we want to convey, but when it comes to expressing it through speaking, something gets lost because of the fear of how it will be perceived. But when you write it down, it may flow more freely and fluently, without fear of being misunderstood or judged. So always have a journal with you when you meditate.

Recipe forMeditation

1) Be honest with yourself about you!

2) Set yourself apart from normal activity; understand that this process is more than separation from daily activities but an opportunity to be one with yourself and your Higher Power, and to receive divine precept for the days to come in your preparation.

3) Dialogue with God is essential to this process, as instructions are the only way of moving forward in every area.

4) Speak what you want and believe. Mantra examples: I am love, I receive love and I give love, I am worthy of love. Love is patient and kind, because I am love. I am patient and kind.

Exercise

Take the time now to write out whatever is concerning you about any area of your life and what you wish to see transformed in this process.

Congratulations, on your first step in the process of preparing for your journey to wholeness. Keep in mind that the process of meditation is not a one-time practice and must become a part of your daily activities. The guidelines I've provided are a way of getting started in the meditation process. As you move forward, you'll receive instructions from your Higher Power on how to meditate and come into the truth of who you are as an individual.

Understand the first month may be challenging, as you have to transition your mind and activities in order to focus on who you are and what you want. A part of this process is to do everything you can to stay focused as you get distracted by people, thoughts, and situations. The first step is typically the hardest, because it requires the most time and attention, and that's when friends want to go to that great party, or the ex you're wanting to separate from will present himself saying all the right things. Watch out for the subtle distractions that seem harmless but will take you completely away from the process. Remember, distractions are outer (other people and circumstances) and inner (fear, impatience). Stay on course as you journey to self-love and fulfillment.

NOTES

Beauty
(Inner and Outer)

In being whole, you must know your beauty and the beauty of the truth you're living in, through meditation. Many women have determined their beauty based on the opinions of others or what they've seen on television or in magazines, and it's been strictly based on outer appearance rather than inner beauty.

I remember once asking a male friend if he thought I was pretty enough for him. In turn I received the most memorable statement. He said, "Many girls are pretty, but many aren't beautiful." He then finished his statement with, "You're pretty but you're not always beautiful," which was a hit in the truth area. Ouch! I have to say I was offended by his statement, so of course I had to ask what he meant. He said, "Pretty girls are just that—pretty on the outside; but beauty is a reflection of the inside that transitions to the outside. Your attitude and character determine your beauty."

When I heard that I was amazed. I had always just looked on the surface making sure my outer appearance was attractive, but not once did I look at my inner beauty to assure it was reflected on the outer. Now I had to meditate on these questions: Do I have a good or bad attitude? What is my general attitude towards people? How do I treat people? Am I as beautiful inside as I am outside?

Some of you should be asking yourself and meditating on the same questions. Ladies, beauty is more than just outer appearance; it includes your inner self as well. We spend so much time with lotions and potions, masks, manicures, pedicures, and hairstyles that we forget to pamper and manicure our inner selves.

I enjoy the scripture that reads: "You were beautifully and wonderfully made." That says to me that we're all naturally beautiful and wonderful, but at times it may be hard to see because of experiences or circumstances. And just as we spend time and care to beautify our outer appearance, we must do the same with the inner by meditating on the truth about ourselves. We need to learn how to let our inner beauty reflect in our outer beauty.

If you've ever seen a lighthouse in the middle of the ocean at night, you'll notice how it shines light on every area it's directed to. Your inner beauty should be just like that light, shining its light on every area of your life. This allows you to see where you're going and what needs to be changed, and it allows you the opportunity to see if everything is in its place (your attitude, conversation, love, treatment of others, etc.).

My girlfriend and I had code words we would say when we were out and men were constantly approaching us: "Our light must be on today." Another scripture reads: "Let your light so shine that men may see your good works and glorify your Father in heaven." Let me say this: when your attitude, your relationship with the Higher Power, and your outer appearance are in sync, then your light will shine bright so men (and women) will see all that is good within and without.

Many times we're fearful of showing our inner beauty due to past hurts and painful circumstances whether through rape, molestation, or failed relationships/ marriage. Whatever your reasoning, you must determine that the fear you carry is a blockage from the true beauty of you. Understand that fear is weakness, and it creates timidness and uncertainty. We must live a life of power, in true beauty, which will keep our minds focused and free.

Growing up I had a skin rash, which always made me self-conscious about my appearance. At times people would complement me, but most of the time the focus was on my skin. Although I was self-conscious, I did my best to maintain my value, until a member of my family told me I wasn't pretty. At that moment, my mind shifted from self-consciousness to low self-esteem. Just by the opinion of another, my confidence was crushed. This is what happens many times: we allow the opinions of others to dictate how we perceive ourselves.

What/Who changed your mind about your beauty?

I love the saying: "Beauty is in the eye of the beholder." Here's some truth about that saying: YOU must be the initial beholder of your beauty. Otherwise you leave the door open for others to dictate your beauty. And no matter what's said, whether a compliment or negative comment, you can only believe what your own eyes see.

Have you ever had someone compliment you on a day when you didn't feel your best or you felt you didn't look your best? That compliment you just received didn't register in your mind because of your own perception of you. Let's reverse that scenario to a day when you got all dolled up and you knew you looked good. At that time it really wouldn't matter who liked or disliked your look, because your perception of you was pure beauty.

And that was based on your perception of what was happening inside you. Yet, there are times when the outer appearance reflects the inner battles or struggles. Understand that what's going on inside will affect your outer appearance and your environment.

I can remember a particular time when I could see that my outer atmosphere was a reflection of what was going on inside. I couldn't keep my house clean. Seemingly it was easier for me to find things in a disorganized mess rather than being organized. Disorganization seemed to be easier, because of the inner disorganization and battle that was going on inside me. There were deep-rooted issues I hadn't dealt with stemming from childhood and continuing into adulthood.

For many years I dealt with daddy issues, as many women do, which caused a lot of my health issues. It was a downward spiral, because as the health concerns progressed, my self-esteem deteriorated with it. With low self-esteem issues came bad eating habits, since I would eat to get over the issues that were bothering me, whether about health, relationships, work, or family. Then came the weight gain that further sent my self-esteem diving off a cliff, and the thought of being beautiful was far from my mind.

My family had no idea how to help me. Their way was to be harsh, thinking that would motivate me to lose weight and take more interest in my appearance. I deal with diet in the next chapter; however, I wanted to show how the downward spiral can affect various areas of your life dealing with beauty.

I came to a place in my mind where I figured that since I was fat and unattractive, there was no point in sprucing up. So I didn't do anything to beautify myself, and hygiene as unladylike as it may sound, depended on whether or not I had somewhere to go.

One definition of beauty is to be excellent, therefore I believe beauty requires excellence. In order for us to walk in beauty, every area of our lives must be excellent—not perfect but excellent. Perfection means there are no flaws or defects, while excellence speaks of quality. In regard to beauty it means the inner (attitude) must be of good quality—not flawless, but good. So since beauty is a reflection of your attitude, and your attitude must be excellent, regardless of what's going on in your life, you must see beauty in it. Maintaining an excellent attitude isn't easy when life hands us difficulties, but the daily challenge will be to wake up and carry out a good attitude no matter what's happening or not happening.

I can recall meeting many women over my lifetime who were gorgeous on the outside, but their attitude was horrible. Nothing was ever going right in their lives, and their viewpoint was being reflected in their outer appearance. They began looking run down and older, and no longer took pride in their appearance. They were the true statement of a bag lady, where you could see the issues of life weighing them down. Remember when women would ask each other if they had bags under their eyes? The reason they asked was because bags under the eyes made them look tired and took away from their beauty.

That's what's happening to many women: failed relationships, abuse (mental, physical, verbal, and emotional), conceit, anger, and bitterness are just a few of the leading causes of spiritual bags that cause beauty to fade and women to become tired mentally, emotionally, spiritually, and physically.

As women we often wonder why we have little energy or motivation. I contend it's due to mental baggage that affects our physical body and surroundings, and these components affect inner and outer beauty. It's time for the beautification process. As I stated earlier, you must get to the root of any issue before you can be free, so the first question I ask is:

What's bothering you? Meditate on this and write down what you hear. You want to recognize and acknowledge what's truly bothering you. Many times as women, we have a problem of holding our feelings and thoughts inside, which doesn't mean we don't talk or vent, but we typically tend to talk and vent about what we don't mind other people knowing. Yet anything of importance we feel we'll be judged on, we tend to keep as a secret and hold inside.

Do you ever get the sense that although someone is speaking to you, they're talking around the subject? The more they talk around the issue, the more difficult it is to understand where they're going as the issue they really want to deal with is never resolved. Understand that if you hold on to an unresolved issue, it becomes like a seed buried in the ground that will grow into a tree.

Many women who have dealt with childhood molestation have been taught to never speak about their experience of hurt, pain, and shame. And in most of these instances, that devastation is like that seed buried in the ground. Because it wasn't addressed, it began to grow like a tree and it took form in the shape of promiscuity, failed relationships, the inability to be affectionate, low self-esteem, fear, and lack of trust to name a few. Can you imagine if those women were able to speak of their pain and hurt, how the negative effects could have possibly been avoided?

You must come to the place where you now ask yourself what's really bothering you and allow yourself to feel whatever's necessary in order to overcome the issue. For many it may just be one matter, but for most of us, it's a lifetime of pain, regrets, and disappointment. Take time to meditate and ask: what's bothering me? Write down what you hear; one thing you can't deny is written words. Writing is therapeutic as it allows your heart to come through and flow freely without hindrances. Know that what's in your heart will come out eventually, and there's no safer place than writing in your journal. Remember, for this to be effective, be true to yourself when answering this question, because if you can't be honest with yourself, how can you be truthful with others? And what's bothering you will never be resolved.

Now that you've discovered and written it down, you must now ask the follow up questions that are more than likely already written down or known. Who caused you the pain? What part did you play in the experience if any? These answers will lead you to your healing, which is through forgiveness.

Forgiveness

Not forgiving will leave you full of bitterness, anger, and strife. The more you allow it in your heart, the darker your surroundings become. In a place of darkness, it's hard to see the light. Many of us are groping in the darkness of our heart because of unforgiveness, which has the ability to prevent every good thing from coming to you. For example, if you've ever been hurt in a relationship and haven't forgiven the person who hurt you, you build a wall with your negative attitude and bitterness which prevents someone who may be able to love you from connecting with you.

Understand in this part of the process, you must decide if you'll hold the person(s) hostage in your thoughts with unforgiveness, or if you'll release them from your mind thus releasing your bitterness. Unforgiveness is the act of holding someone prisoner in your mind based on what they've done to you. It's easier to hold them to the wrong, and you probably have every right to charge them as guilty, because in your mind to forgive means they're innocent of all charges.

How do you forgive someone who has intentionally hurt you and has made no apologies? You do it for you—not them! You learn how not to allow the offense of someone else to set in your heart, because once it sets in, bitterness creeps in as well. Many times the person who caused the offense may not care that they've harmed you; however, in other cases they may not even be aware that they've offended you. While you live in bitterness, anger, and unforgiveness, they're out living their lives connecting with new relationships.

We may assume that the person who caused the offense won't be able to be happy, which isn't true. As you discover the cause and identify who inflicted the hurt, the next steps are like the layers of the Wedding Cake—it depends on you and how many layers you're willing to go in forgiveness. In my experience, I've been offended and hurt in many relationships. And I've been the offender in some instances and needed forgiveness. Yet in most cases, regardless of what the circumstances were in those relationships, I've been able to speak my hurts, concerns, and regrets and move past the incidences.

Although, I'm reminded of one particular relationship with my then fiancé, who while we were together asked another woman to marry him. When I became aware of their relationship and the betrayal, I was extremely hurt, but I moved on without addressing the matter, or the hurt and pain I experienced. I didn't take the opportunity to deal with my anger, and years later, when I saw the woman I considered a home wrecker, I was furious and determined to give her hell for the pain she caused me.

When I approached her, the only thing I could see was a hurting person. Many hurting people are hurting others because of their own emptiness, bitterness, and anger. Hurt, pain, and unforgiveness has a way of creeping up at the most inopportune time, which is why it's so important to acknowledge. That seed of anger and bitterness will destroy relationships that are intended to bring you love and a beautiful life, yet will ultimately destroy you and your spirit. Unforgiveness keeps people from trusting and loving and causes them to block any good from coming in, because they're wallowing in anger and victim mentality.

Why are you holding on to unforgiveness? We often hold on because we think it gives us power over the person who has caused the pain and hurt. Or we feel as though if we release it, we'll have nothing else to hold on to, therefore we're left with no options but to be vulnerable. I've spoken to many women who stated that they're attached to their bitterness, because they didn't receive an apology from the person who caused their pain.

Know that you may never receive the apology you're hoping for, for various reasons, but you can seek forgiveness. Forgiveness doesn't come when someone apologizes; it comes from within, with or without an apology. Forgiveness is the act of YOU freeing your heart and soul from any offense that's keeping you hostage from moving forward. You won't experience inner beauty—and therefore outer beauty—until you release past hurts and offer forgiveness!

Exercise

1) Begin by acknowledging the hurt (yes they hurt you, and you have every right to feel the way you do). Keep in mind, the acknowledgment of hurt doesn't give you the right to play victim to gain power over anyone.

2) Determine within your heart that you'll release the person who hurt you. Then say in your heart and aloud that this is the last time

you'll speak of the incident or person in a negative manner.

3) For those who are interested in a higher level or tier just like on the Wedding Cake, know that complete forgiveness comes by confessing to yourself and the person who offended you. If you're able, depending on your situation, pick up the phone, send an email, or meet with the person and let them know you forgive them.

4) The final act you must now take is to forgive yourself, as the unforgiveness of others has kept you dormant from relationships because of lack of trust, which has affected you financially, emotionally, spiritually, and physically. As you go through the process of forgiveness, you'll begin to notice the difference in your relationships, your conversations, and even your mental and physical health—as well as your inner and outer beauty. Your daily activities and life events will become lighter as you now have an understanding of how to recognize when unforgiveness is setting in, and you have the knowledge of how to forgive and move

forward. Forgiveness is but one path to letting your inner beauty shine outward.

NOTES

Diet
(A Healthy Lifestyle)

Over the years I've experimented with many diets and have failed at attempting to lose weight a significant number of times. I'm an emotional eater (sound familiar?), which means I eat when I'm happy, sad, angry, depressed—any emotion will do. How much I consume depends on the situation.

You need to realize that diet often refers to what you eat, not necessarily trying to lose weight, and it's an important component of living a life of wholeness. See, if you're unhealthy in your body, it's difficult to be healthy in your mind.

In this chapter I'll address two components of dieting: the physical diet that results in the release of unwanted body weight and the emotional diet that results in the release of unhealthy/unattainable relational desires. Often women go for the bad boy or the unattainable married man, even though there's a neon light that says "off limits." Just like the sugar temptation, it's about wanting something that's off limits.

The attraction to the married man is sometimes because the woman knows this man doesn't mind commitment or long term relationships. But the reality is just because he isn't opposed to commitment doesn't mean he wants to be committed to his mistress. Women don't comprehend that if the unattainable married man is engaging in infidelity, he isn't really committed to anyone. If he were, the idea of being with someone other than his wife (committed partner) would never happen. What occurs in these instances—like dieting—is when you're told you can't or shouldn't have something, you're naturally more attracted to that which is off limits.

The consensus of many diets typically says that to lose weight you have to take away something you're craving or love to maximize the results you desire. That isn't always easy, just as maintaining a healthy diet—even after you've lost the weight—isn't simple. For example, do you ever affirm that you're giving up bread, but the day you make that decision all the temptations present themselves wherever you go. The lure is hard to resist because of the idea you put in your mind that you couldn't have bread.

Now many who've experienced dieting know that once you've satisfied the craving, continuous consumption becomes redundant, unsatisfying, and many times disgusting. It's the same with the unattainable married man or bad boy: he cheats, becomes verbally abusive, acts disrespectful, loses interest, and in some cases become physically violent.

Women who haven't determined their value become desperate for companionship and will sacrifice their integrity and worth for the unattainable—which won't last. We've sought many ways to maintain the unattainable such as spending countless dollars or giving our bodies over to a man. How do I know? I was one of many women who used money, spoiling, and giving my body in sex to obtain and maintain the unattainable. The idea behind these behaviors is that we think we need to show our value, rather than knowing we're of value and allowing others to see that value—in appropriate ways.

Many young women today think sex is a way of showing love and value, not realizing that men won't know their value or commit to them based on sex. Women have to learn to change their emotional diet, which means changing their manner of living. Some have been living a certain way for so long, it seems impossible to change, but I will show you how.

Consumption is the key to changing your manner of living. So I ask: What are you consuming? How much are you consuming? When are you consuming? If you want to live a healthy, whole life, you need to consider the foods you eat, the conversations you have, the relationships you're in, and the thoughts that enter your mind.

It's important to learn to consume what's healthy for your fulfillment. As you've seen, the process toward being whole begins with meditation, then focusing on your inner beauty, and next forgiveness. One of my greatest resources, the Bible, contains a scripture that talks about meditating and consuming what's true, worthy of reverence (deep respect) and honor, pure, lovely, kind, and excellent.

What in your life contains those attributes? That's what you must consume and focus on. If you're able to consume the beauty of those good qualities, you'll see your manner of living change and shift to a higher level of existence.

Many women don't realize the importance of what they consume. For example, have you ever heard of someone going through hard times in their relationship maybe because someone is cheating? Unknowingly, just by hearing about this, you've consumed that conversation which causes your imagination to run amok. You might start to analyze your relationship based on that conversation which wasn't even affecting you directly. Or you may make judgments about the people in that relationship.

You must learn to filter what you hear and see, and even the places you go. My great resource says to guard your heart with all diligence because from the heart flows the issues of life. Understand that what you consume abundantly will come out eventually and affect your lifestyle. So ensure that you're consuming only positive influences.

After learning to adopt the lifestyle of a healthy mind and thought process by knowing your value—your emotional diet—we next need to deal with a healthy lifestyle through your physical diet—what you eat!

Ladies, it's time to get healthy in mind as well as body to have a lifestyle of wholeness, so let's talk about eating consumption. Recognize that skipping breakfast, munching unhealthy snacks, and eating fast food is training the body to crave an unnatural, unhealthy way of living. My understanding is that as women we're extremely emotional and similar to a drug addict when trying to soothe pain or escape from reality. We use food (rather than drugs) as a way of coping with our emotions.

On many occasions I've used emotions as an excuse to justify my eating habits. Now some women actually know how to maintain a healthy diet but have no motivation to exercise or be active. And others may enjoy being active, but have poor eating habits. However, in both cases, the excuses are evident. How many excuses have you used? Too tired! Too lonely! Too bored! Too anxious!

Just eating right doesn't produce healthy living, just as believing in a dream doesn't produce results without corresponding action. Eating healthy food and keeping your body in motion are the formula for a healthy body. You need to discover what's comfortable for you, since each exercise and diet isn't for everyone. We're all unique in every way.

Earlier I stated that you must get to know yourself, what makes you tick. So now, ask yourself these questions to help you understand yourself a little better. What causes you to overeat? What emotions make you eat certain foods? What foods would you say you're addicted to? These questions are essential to moving forward in healthy living, because the more you know yourself, the more aware you become of your eating habits and actions.

And, you must learn to be accountable for your actions, as no one can keep you accountable but you. You spend more time with you than anyone else, so as you begin to understand what makes you act or react, you can then keep yourself on track and accountable.

Remember the **key components for a healthy lifestyle for your mind and body** are:

1) Consumption (healthy thoughts and healthy food)

2) Accountability (do what you say you'll do)

3) Exercise (find a way to move your body that you enjoy)

I'm reminded of a particular day when I was working in an office and my coworkers were scrabbling around to prepare themselves for work that should have already been completed. On a typical day, everyone was relaxed and unbothered by the work that needed to be done; however on this day, I couldn't understand their actions. So I asked a coworker about the new activity that was making everyone so frantic. I was told the District Supervisor was on his way to the office. Now in my mind their actions seemed foolish and unnecessary, so I continued my daily activity unbothered and unmoved by the thought of the supervisor coming in to observe.

The question here is: Why did I not become frantic like the others? It was due to knowledge I gained at an early age: if you take every necessary precaution to assure you're accountable for what's assigned to you, there's no need for worry or stress when met with challenges and evaluations.

Women are so good at hiding behind their masks that many times, just like those workers, they have an illusion of their daily activity, knowing once the boss (their accountability) leaves they'll return to their mundane activities. Women, as your own boss, you must hold yourself accountable to begin and maintain the healthy manner of living for mind, body, and spirit.

As women, we're guilty of attempting to live a better, complete existence, but due to those excuses we revert back to what's familiar—that unhealthy lifestyle consuming all the wrong, negative things from relationships to ideas to food. Why is it so easy to regress back to the familiar or unhealthy manner of living? It's because we live in a popcorn world where many expect things to just happen, and when results or solutions are slow to arrive, discouragement and impatience set in, especially when genuine effort has been put forth.

Other times when results are evident, many women think they no longer have to be accountable, and that becomes their opportunity to take time out. Concerning your lifestyle, there's never a time to slack off, because the moment you do is the moment the work you've put in begins to shift. It's a daily commitment to healthy eating, moderate activity, and positive thoughts to maintain a fulfilling life.

What happens in many relationships is they start off fine, and somewhere in there comfort sets in and one person stops doing what's necessary to maintain the relationship. And typically most times in these relationships when things go south, women sacrifice what they think will get the relationship back. Some will sacrifice their bodies, finances, or spirituality, not understanding that there's no part of you that can be separated when sacrificing.

Here's what I mean: as women you weren't built to give your body and your mind and not have the heart follow. You're equipped to be whole. However, you must tap into your inner being for the whole you to manifest into reality. Many women feel empty, broken, and alone and may feel they have every right to throw in the towel. If you're that woman, I encourage you to not throw in the towel on life, because there's something on the inside of you that enforces that hope of wholeness.

Recipe

For a healthy diet mentally and physically

1) Consumption. Watch what you're consuming (conversations, friendships, relationships, food, ideas...)

2) Accountability. Be accountable to yourself first. Understand you're the only person you must answer to, because when you look back over the years, either you'll be proud or live in regret— just know the choice is yours.

3) Exercise. Work out whatever in your life causes you to be stagnant and unproductive if you desire to become who you want to be and to get to where you want to go—which is whole and fulfilled. Learn to exercise self-control, patience, and the ability to give what you can and receive from others what they're willing to share. Most of

all guard your heart from negativity that has the ability to derail your process toward wholeness.

Exercise 1

Write in your journal and ask yourself these questions:

1) What is causing me to be stagnant in my life?

2) What can I actively do to change my environment to create a drama-free, stress-free zone?

3) How can I get on a healthy path emotionally, spiritually, financially, and physically?

Eating and Getting Active for Wholeness

When attaining a healthy body, you must be aware that you're unique from other women, and what worked for another may not work for you. However, the formula is the same: *change the way you're eating and move your body*. For example, if your challenge is portion control, reduce your portions from large to medium or small. You know your body better than anyone, so you have to be the driving force in this process.

I was aware that my primary food issue was portion control, and I loved junk food, especially potato chips. And I loved eating late at night. When I began my process to become healthy, what I first I needed to tackle was to stop eating after 7 pm. This took a month to adapt to. After my body was used to that, I begin to consume less food. Notice I didn't say I deprived myself of anything I wanted to eat. I just knew that whatever I consumed must be in a smaller portion and eaten before 7 pm.

During this process I began to see the results of my efforts, and the more results I saw the more I wanted to be an active participant in my health. I've never been one to exercise or be active in any way besides dancing on occasion. But what I discovered is when I made the decision to get active and take walks, I was able to rid my mind of frustration, stress, and worry. This was also a time of meditation for me. And then I realized those occasions when I was dancing could be implemented into my lifestyle change. So no longer did I wait for a party or a night out to dance; I put on some music and danced away my worries and extra pounds in my living room!

The results of being active were so motivating that I knew the next step had to be taken in changing my manner of living. Although I hadn't changed anything I was eating, on this journey my body began to crave healthier foods. In place of sugar treats, I ate fruit. In place of chips and dip, I craved carrots or celery dipped in hummus. This change started in my thoughts during times of meditation, which created the determination to become a healthier woman. The results were evident in the lost weight, but more importantly, they were evident in my belief that anything I set out to change can be done—with motivation, determination, and meditation.

The formula for health is: portion control, exercise, water, stress reduction, and healthy eating. The uniqueness of the formula is the order in which you decide to follow your process. Each topic will be unique to you as well depending on your preferences.

Exercise 2

Before you start the journey toward a healthy lifestyle, find out if you're an emotional eater. What foods do you crave for each emotion: happy, sad, depressed, lonely, or excited? Once you've answered these questions, take your first step, whichever you decide to start with. For example, with portion control, if you're a late night eater, give yourself a schedule of when you'll eat your last meal that would be earlier than usual. Snacking is great but can be harmful to weight loss if you're consuming large meals and snacks in between, especially high calorie snacks at night. Limit your snacks, and choose more sensible, smaller snacks if you're eating large meals, until you conquer portion control.

The ultimate goal is to reduce your portions until your body understands when it's satisfied rather than overindulging for the feeling of fullness. If you're like I was and the thought of getting active is far from your mind, begin by doing something you love to do. If you're near a beach and that's where you love to be, take a walk and enjoy the scenery. Relax your thoughts as you're walking, as a relaxed mind is not on a time tracker. The more you become active and choose this as a time to meditate as well, it becomes a time of serenity and peace rather than just exercise.

Cleaner/healthier eating depends on your preferences. Although we've been told by doctors and popular media that fruits and vegetables are the healthiest, I believe cleaner/healthier eating depends on the individual. If you're a sugar treat eater, and you choose to not consume that any longer because of the lasting effects it may have on you, that in itself is healthier eating. You might learn to appease your sweet tooth with fresh fruits.

Many of us are unaware of the effects of stress and how it affects weight loss especially in women. It will serve you in so many ways to learn to reduce your stress intake. The more you're able to release stress—and meditation helps here—the greater results you'll witness in improved health in body and mind.

With all the dietary tips available, if changing your lifestyle is important, you have no excuses. Determine what works for you based on the topics in the formula. Is it necessary to spend money to lose weight? Not really. Know that this isn't just about losing a few pounds, rather it's about making a lifestyle change. If spending money will help you change your manner of living, that's your decision to make. For example, if you wanted to hire a personal trainer to help you exercise and keep you accountable, consider that option. Just keep in mind the amazing and lasting results that come from a changed/renewed mind and a healthy body!

NOTES

Relaxation (Inside and Outside)

When I think of relaxation my mind typically thinks of palm trees, sun, hammocks, and a nice fruity cocktail. Your relaxation may be quite different from mine, but regardless of the scenery it delivers the same effect: the feeling of sheer bliss, a moment you can breathe freely, and is virtually anxiety free.

In the process of attaining wholeness you must adopt relaxation as another key component. It's necessary for you to be dedicated and determined to do this, as women have the natural ability to stay busy with too many activities and issues and are constantly moving. You need relaxation in your life, because the spiritual energy (inside you) is the energy reflected in your reality (outside you). I remember as a kid I would hold a magnifying glass over an ant in the sun, and because the reflection of the sun was coming directly through the magnifying glass, the energy of the sun's rays would cause the ant to draw up and burn.

Many women have failed to realize the anxiety they operate in is causing their relationships and various areas of their life to draw up and burn like the ant. The effects of not relaxing can be detrimental to your progress, since the opposite of relaxation includes anxiety, worry, and stress which create havoc in various areas in your manner of living. One way you contribute to the detriment of relaxation is through the words that come out of your mouth. If you constantly say you're tired or burned out, you create that environment with your words.

I'll never forget in 2009 I was homeless, carless, jobless, and needless to say there was less in my life than I would have preferred. At that lowest point I decided to make a change. I was unclear of how to begin the process, but I knew at least I wanted better health. So I chose to focus on what was most important to me at the time: my health. I figured if I was in good health nothing would be impossible. I found a health food store where I could get the necessary supplements I thought would help me build my health.

As I was exiting the store a colorful map caught my attention. I picked it up to see what it was and saw "Feng Shui Made Easy." I read the content and thought I might purchase it. But because of my lack of understanding of Feng Shui, I figured as a Christian this would be like a betrayal of my religion. In my upbringing I was taught the only true knowledge comes from the church.

Women, as a side note: follow your heart, as ideas you may have been taught growing up might not always be as they seem.

When I checked out of the store, I thought about my life and current situation—all that was less than what I wanted—and decided to follow my heart and purchase the Feng Shui map. I started reading about Feng Shui, and to my surprise I found it shared some Biblical principles I had grown up with and believed in. It explained the nine areas of the home or office which require organization and order, but most importantly I found it included meditation and affirmation.

After reading what was necessary to begin my Feng Shui process, I started cleaning and organizing, discarding those items that were no longer necessary for me to hold on to. This was exhilarating, as once everything was clean, organized, and rooms were emptied, it created an atmosphere of peace. (At the time, I was living with my mom.) It's easier to be relaxed when your surroundings are organized, just as it's easier to be relaxed when you mind is clear and free of stress.

Some women are so full of negativity, stress, and baggage, they have no room for anything else in their lives. They're full of drama and work-related duties, family responsibilities, church work, and productive and nonproductive relationships. They're full of what others have told them is necessary, until there's no room for their desires.

I've learned over the years of my process that balance is the key to the wholeness journey. If you don't have balance, one area of your life will get more attention than the others causing neglect, which ultimately affects every area. In the art of Feng Shui, after you've emptied, cleaned, and organized your natural house (environment), you need to apply the same process to your mental, emotional, spiritual, and physical wholeness. This will require you to quiet yourself (process of emptiness) and then speak positively (process of refilling). Speaking or affirming a declaration of your desires is one of the main components in renewing your thoughts and emotions.

Regardless of your religious beliefs, one of the constants in most religions is "What you speak is what you receive," unless you're a monk and have taken a vow of silence. And even then their thought process produces results. Yet for most women, it's necessary for us to talk our way through, so you must watch what comes out of your mouth. We sometimes talk just to figure a solution to a problem, but we have to be careful that we only speak what we want to manifest.

As you change the way you speak and affirm, you'll notice a change in your environment. When I had less in my life, I found that the more I spoke positively, the more it changed the way I thought, and as my thoughts changed my actions changed. I was no longer jobless, carless, or homeless. My life was being filled with great things I had spoken into existence. Women, you have the power to make things happen in every area of your life, but you must tap into a place of discovery—through relaxation.

I can remember speaking an affirmation of love, because that was one of my greatest desires; it simple read: "I am love, I receive love, I am worthy of love, and am able to give love." The purpose of that affirmation was to counter the mindset I had for many years that I must not be worthy of love since I never received it in relationships with the opposite sex. I didn't realize the power I carried, and the more negative I thought the more negative I spoke which affected my results.

There's a scripture that states: "Now, faith is the substance of things hoped for, the evidence of things not seen." Then it goes on to say: "Faith comes by hearing." That means that for faith to be attained and to see evidence, there must be consistent hearing, and in order to hear, someone must be speaking. So understand women that faith speaks what it wants to see and produces evidence. Without knowledge of the words being spoken, you can hear positive words come toward you and not know how to put them into action.

Another of my favorite scriptures reads: "For as the rain and the snow come down from the heaven and do not return there but water the earth, making it bring forth and sprout, giving seed to the sower and bread to the eater. So shall my word which goes forth from my mouth, it shall not return to Me void, but it shall accomplish what I please. And it shall prosper in the matter for which I sent it."

Simply put, God created the earth with mere words, and if He created you, you to have the same power to speak what you desire into existence—whether good or bad. Of course, you may not manifest "bad" things on purpose, but when you say something like "he'll be the death of me" what do you think you might manifest? Just remember: your words are powerful and will produce what you speak. So the ultimate question I have for you is: What are you speaking? Whether in happiness, sadness, joy, sorrow, gladness, or frustration, you must be deliberate with what comes out of your mouth. Your words are a life portal, because whatever proceeds from your mouth is given life.

If you believe in God or a Higher Power, then know that He who created you is a part of you, therefore you have also inherited that same ability as the creator. With that understanding, when you now speak, speak consciously, intentionally, and for a purpose. Stop saying things aren't working, or you never meet a nice guy, or your life isn't where you want it to be, because your life portal is giving life to those very words. You carry greatness inside you, so be aware what speak—because what you speak abundantly and you believe immensely will produce inevitably. A relaxed mind and body are essential for being a positive force for manifesting good in your life.

Faith is what you believe, which includes action.

Recipe

Speak. Faith

Believe. What you're speaking.

Don't doubt. Even when you're frustrated and life doesn't seem to be progressing as you would like it to be in your time.

Stay consistent. Don't change your speaking to match your situation. Speak what you desire to change your situation.

NOTES

Career (And Life Purpose)

The definition of career is an occupation one works at for a significant period of their life with opportunities for progress. I'm not going to discuss getting a job, as most people get one to pay their bills or because they think they're supposed to get a job. A large number of people spend half their lives in a job they hate, yet fool themselves and call it a career. Allow me to be the first to inform you that if you're in a job you hate, it's not a career, and it won't create an opportunity for advancement. Understand that what you hate you're not motivated by, and with no motivation or enthusiasm there's little effort, and you won't do your job effectively. This means when it's time for a promotion you'll be consistently looked over.

Here's a quick test to see if you have a job or career: Do you arrive at work on time? Are you pleasant when you arrive? Do you like your boss? Do you complain about the office and the people in it? These are just a few questions to help you determine whether you're in a job or career. Many people spend a part of their life in school and the other part in a job whether they hate it, love it, or need it. It's because they haven't discovered what they want to do in life.

When I began to meditate, I found that purpose and career go hand in hand. Purpose is what you're created for, something you can't help but do even if you didn't want to because it's part of you. I've spent half of my life figuring out what I should do as a career. As a little girl, I dreamed of being in the entertainment business. I participated in plays and musicals while in high school, and then reality hit me with four words that guided my life, positively or negatively: "You need a job."

In my mind and spirit, all I ever wanted to do was entertain and there was no way at that time a job and entertainment would coincide. So I became the person who conformed to my surroundings, and my course of study in college became job related. It's possible for many to attend college with a major that has little or nothing to do with a potential career as much as it has to do with getting a job.

My mother is a hard worker and great teacher, and I learned from the best how to survive in this world. So I figured if she loved teaching I would try it too. I went to college and studied what my mom studied, which made her extremely proud that I was following in her footsteps. Although I knew my mom would be proud of whatever I chose to do, I thought she expected me to use her as an example. Caution: I urge you to be careful that you're not living your life to make someone else proud or happy, because ultimately you won't be living for you.

Needless to say I didn't finish school, because I wasn't motivated to be a teacher. Let's be realistic: what you're not motivated in, you won't complete or follow through in. So after college I took a job which I believed would lead me into a career; however, I wasted years in employment that led me nowhere. Why didn't this job work for me and turn into a career like it did for so many others? The difference between you and the next woman on the job who's climbing the career ladder is they're motivated by following their purpose. Women must understand that when you love something, you're motivated to pursue it.

Becoming whole doesn't allow you to live off the accomplishments of others and expect to live a life of complete bliss. In this process it's necessary to live your purpose to be successful.

Lots of people equate success as the manifestation of an outcome. Rarely is it equated to the effort that was carried out, whether the outcome was successful or not. Success is having the courage to create a blueprint before you pursue a career, because without the blueprint there would be no building or structure.

Allow me to take this time to applaud you on your current success, as it began the moment you picked up this book to read. This process is not an easy task, and many won't take the opportunity to progress for a variety of reasons, including fear of failure or adverse results. Often successful people will tell you that there were countless failures before their success, and it was the failures that helped them succeed. Let me just say I believe it wasn't the failures that caused them to succeed, but the thought of success (after the failures) that caused the accomplished outcomes.

When I began my journey to wholeness, my constant thoughts were on the end results of success. I gave no thought to the beginning, middle, or the challenges I would face. I'd hear several leaders say that God shows you the end result of something, because if He showed you the beginning and the in-between process you would probably not move forward and would give up before you began.

Through my meditation I realized God's intent for us is to win, to succeed. Therefore He wouldn't show us anything discouraging, because the end result we've been shown is the success. Oftentimes the purpose of seeing the outcome in your imagination is so your mind can be transformed to success. Imagine if you were a boxer and you knew you were going to win a fight. The way you enter the ring would be much different that if you thought you would lose. You'd enter with confidence and no fear of failure. This is how you must live your life of fulfillment: knowing that the end result is certain and lacking nothing in mind, emotion, and spirit, but receiving purposed success.

Numerous women spend their lives wanting to be something other than what they are. Either you know who you are or you don't. But you must understand that the attempts to be someone other than who you are will create frustration and further diminish your self-confidence and self-worth. I find women get discouraged, depressed, or angry because they haven't discovered their true identities or purpose on earth. And others are angry because they're unable to fill a role that wasn't intended for them, so they're hiding behind the identity of another.

The reason we hide behind false identities is that we figure if the people we're modeling are successful, we'll have the same results. The fear of success and fear of failure is too much for many to cope with, which is why some attempt to pattern themselves after others. However, a lot of people have failed to understand that every path of success is different, just as each one of us has unique fingerprints. It's the same with success: the goal is the same; however, my success will be much different than yours, though the formula is similar.

The fear of failure is a part of the process of success; the key is to not allow the failure to shape your mind on the outcome. Understand that without failure it's generally impossible to know success. Like in baking a cake, if you never had one come out flat, hard, or tasteless, you would never know the success of the perfect cake.

In business and relationships I've had many ups and downs, but without the downs I would have been unable to recognize the ups. Success to me is as simple as waking up in the morning, because it means I have another opportunity to move toward the end result of success in every endeavor.

Many say try and try again until you succeed, yet you've probably heard that trying doesn't constitute doing; it's only repeating an action that hasn't worked. If the act of trying had produced results before there would be no need to try again. Another opportunity to move forward means no longer wallowing, settling, or forcing something to work that didn't work before. Moving forward means you're making the choice to revamp, re-access, and move toward the thought of the successful results.

I've had the opportunity to speak with countless women, and they speak of failure in relationships; this thinking sends them into depression, complacency, and loneliness. My job in advising them in these matters is for them to look at what they consider a failure as a learning tool, not a time to give up or even try again, but a reflection in order to re-access and not succumb to the same results.

In my relationships I would consistently have one failed one after another. I couldn't understand why they were failing and had no answers to allow me the opportunity to make the necessary changes. It would take for me to begin my process of wholeness to understand that each relationship was a stepping stone or learning tool to a successful life of fulfillment. I learned through each experience what I liked and disliked, what made me happy and refilled my spirit, and I determined to take the initiative in my life.

Many women are waiting for someone to make them happy and bring joy in their lives, when they haven't discovered what makes them tick. I need you to understand that if you haven't discovered who you are, what your purpose is, and what success means for you, you'll continue in the cycle of failure. In each failed relationship, I was able to access each individual and choose the characteristics I liked and desired in a relationship, not that I would attain them all in one person, but I knew what I wanted. The true success of a failed relationship is the ability to recognize your needs and desires and focus your mind on the ability to be whole. Just as the true success of a rewarding career is finding your purpose and pursuing it.

Recipe

1) **Acceptance:** Accept that failure is inevitable.

2) **Determination**: Determine to learn from failure in order to move forward and succeed.

3) **Recognition**: Recognize the course of action that needs to change in order to not repeat failure.

4) **Understand**: Success is not the end of something but the determination to transform your mind and move toward a full life.

Exercise

Make the necessary efforts to move forward in your career. If you're a singer, create a demo, or make calls on your behalf. Create an avenue to be recognized, and even if it doesn't work the first time, keep taking steps until you know you've given it your everything—that's success.

NOTES

Love
(Of Self and Others)

I had little perception of love throughout my life. I heard the words but had no understanding of what they meant. My mom would say, "I love you" and my dad would utter those same words, but one parent was there to supply my needs and desires, while the other was gone and stopped in periodically. However, when my father did come to spend time with me, I would end up at my grandmother's house where I heard those same words and was allowed to have my own way. So my perception of love as I matured was that love supplies needs and desires, and it will leave, reject you, make false promises—and let you have your own way.

A lot of women have grown up with a similar perception, whether recognized or not. Ever wonder why women relate money and gifts to love? It's because someone who gave them gifts used those same words. Another form of love that's misinterpreted is sex; however, it's the most used act of love that confuses so many minds.

I learned some time ago that love is a faith word, which is something believed and accompanied with action in the belief. Love should operate in an unconditional state. It's not an "if, then" word, meaning "if" love does this "then" I'll respond this way. I know women have heard the words "I love you" and reacted with the only action they related to those words, which was sex.

I was taught that behind every action taken or word spoken there's an intention. For some the main intention behind the words "I love you" is to get something in return, rather than unconditional intentions. Let's examine the unconditional love you hopefully have for yourself: there's no length you wouldn't go to make yourself happy and take care of you. For example, if there was a dress or a piece of jewelry you wanted, you wouldn't say to yourself, "if" you loved me "then" you would buy me this dress or piece of jewelry. Because of your love for yourself, you make yourself happy without thought or intent. Whether you succeeded on a diet, got a promotion, or lost your job, you move into the action of loving yourself without thought. That's what love does—it moves into action without thought and speaks without intent— unconditionally. I hope this is true for you, because if you want to understand unconditional love, you have to start with yourself!

Unfortunately, some women haven't yet realized they deserve unconditional love. They spend countless dollars and waste time trying again and again to attain unconditional love without ever understanding what love means and does. I encounter women who haven't loved themselves, because of the false perceptions and deceptions subjected on them by those who didn't understand true love. These women think their hair length, cup size, or jean size will help them get the love they desire. However, that's the false perception of love.

The love you're seeking is within you, and until you're able to recognize and receive that love from within, there's no way you'll experience true love (unconditional love). You must understand that the love you can't recognize is the love you'll never know, because how can you have something you haven't experienced? This is why so many relationships fail: because typically women ask the other person to give them love that they have no knowledge of. Again, you first need to know of unconditional love by loving yourself unconditionally and demonstrating it with your words and actions.

I want you to be aware that unconditional love doesn't want its own way; however, it's kind and unselfish. As women think love has a different path than that of meditation and forgiveness, I remind them that love has the same goal, which is to serve in the journey to wholeness. Love knows what it needs, even if an individual doesn't, and it may not match up with our desires. Everything you need is inside you, and there's a part of you that knows exactly what you need. That's love.

Oftentimes we have difficulty yielding to what's inside us, because of our lack of confidence due to the poor choices we've made because we didn't listen to the voice within. Now whether you're Christian or not, I'm sure you've heard this principle—one of the greatest commandments: to love others as you love yourself. So many people don't know how to love themselves which is why they don't know how to love others. I don't think we understand that love is an action word.

I had no understanding what true love was, so I was grateful that during my time of meditation my mantra was "I am love, I receive love, I know how to give love." I came to believe that the more I focused my mind on love, the more it would come from within me. And it did spring forth, because as it was my focus, I began to have faith and acted upon love. I started to show love to the unloving, and I treated and loved others as I desired to be treated and loved. When referring to the command, "love others as you love yourself," you must become self-centered. Automatically "self-centered" probably makes you think you're focusing solely on yourself and your own concerns and that you're selfish. But what I'm referring to is being centered in your thoughts—to know how you want to be loved in order to love others in that same manner.

During one of the most difficult times in my life, I learned that loving myself is the most important love I could give. At times I said I loved myself, yet although I believed that statement was true, it was only a phrase I used and not an action. I was constantly saying I loved myself, but I allowed others to use, abuse, and mistreat my love. Understand women, that anyone who uses your love to benefit themselves and doesn't return their love isn't worthy of your love.

Never once did I question my actions of loving those who didn't return or appreciate the love I gave. I was always looking to understand why my love was being mistreated and abused. The simple truth was I didn't love myself enough to make a change in my choice of whom to love.

During times of failed relationships, women often ask themselves why their love wasn't enough for the other individual. I believe that the love they gave wasn't enough for them. Typically the love women give is the love they want to receive. The frustration comes when the love they give isn't returned in the manner in which they want to receive it. If women loved themselves the way they love others—even those undeserving—there would be no deficiencies within them. This is where self-worth is birthed—through the love you show and give to yourself. I love the phrase that says: "We teach others how to treat us." We do this by the love we choose to give or not give to ourselves.

As women we're created full of love; however, life's circumstances have shown and taught us bitterness, discontent, and settling for less which has resulted in low self-esteem. As part of the preparation to fulfillment, you have to be an active participant of all areas of your life, including those mentioned in the previous chapters.

As I'm sure you've noticed, I'm a believer in God and His word, and I know the greatest of all commandments is love. This commandment states that the only way others will know you're a believer is through the love you show, not just to others but to yourself. I acknowledged these words about love, but in my earlier years my understanding wasn't in its full maturity. I knew that I should treat others with love in order to show God's love, but I didn't understand that same love must begin with me.

Many people have said when they met me, how nice, kind, and loving I am; however, they didn't know that when I left their presence, the love I was showing others, I wasn't giving myself. My love had never extended to myself until I learned the love I was giving needed to start with me. I know you may be wondering how to love yourself. May I suggest that it needs to start in your thought process? You may not realize that what you think of consistently is what will manifest in your mind and reality. At least until you read this book!

Women, you must fill your mind with an abundance of love, and you can only do this by watching what you consume mentally, emotionally, and spiritually. What you read in books, watch on television, or listen to on the radio—and even in some conversations—play a major role in the thought process of love. You must also be mindful of what you say, because you want your atmosphere to be filled with life-giving, love-filled, powerful words.

Oftentimes whatever's happening in our immediate environment is what we speak of. For example, if there's an argument going on, every thought in your mind is negative and you speak words that may cause remorse—and certainly not the results you desire. You must not allow your environment to state how you react or how you show love to yourself or others. I know women who are and have been in relationships that dictated the love they showed themselves based on how someone else felt about them. Understand when you give another individual a portion of control over your love and how and when you give and receive it, you end up like a bank account with insufficient funds—no ability to withdraw what you need, and what you deposit will be depleted to cover the deficit.

There becomes an imbalance unless women understand that the love they give themselves will be the love they receive from others. It's not that others will always give you what you give yourself, but it's a changed mind with the understanding that the love and treatment others give must match your standards. And if it doesn't measure up, then don't settle for less than you give yourself. I know, you're waiting for and probably dependent upon a man to give you the love you desire. But you haven't yet received the knowledge that self-love determines what you're willing to accept and receive from another. Now you have that knowledge!

Over the years, I've learned that if you're determined to be in a loving relationship, you must first have a loving relationship with yourself. That's the secret! You don't have to search all over to obtain the love you have on the inside. The question is: How can you recognize the love you desire if you haven't recognized the love within? It's only a matter of getting real with yourself and acknowledging that the love you thought you were giving yourself isn't enough. If it were you wouldn't feel any deficiencies or lack in that area.

A part of loving yourself requires recognizing your likes and dislikes, discovering your assets and flaws. Even loving your flaws is a part of the process of wholeness, because you might be allowing the dislike of your flaws to dictate the love you give and receive. How many women have questioned their flaws as the reason for the end of a relationship? For example, my hair wasn't long enough, my eyelashes weren't curly enough, I was too overweight, etc. You must find the good in you, what you can love no matter what others may think. If you don't find the good in the flaw or quirk, and if someone comes along with a compliment, you won't accept it because of your self-perception, which makes it hard to receive the praise.

Something I learned from a friend is that you must appreciate yourself and the effort you put into loving yourself and others, whether it's acknowledged or not. Let me explain why she felt the need to express this to me. At that time I had difficulty receiving love and compliments, even as I was able to give them to others. Now the reasons I had such a tough time receiving were I was almost always the giver, and every negative experience in my life, or flaw, or what someone spoke negatively about me dictated my judgment and perception of myself.

One day my friend gave me a compliment, and in a shy, disapproving manner I rejected it. As she wanted to build my confidence, she asked, "When you look in the mirror after you get dressed, do you think you're pretty?" My reply was, "Of course." Her follow up comment would change my thinking. She said, "If it weren't your intention to look good, you wouldn't have used the mirror, and you left the mirror with a look with which YOU were pleased, with or without the approval of someone else."

Therefore my understanding when receiving a compliment is that the giver of the compliment is only reflecting what you see in the mirror. People around you will only mirror your thoughts and actions, the way you see and treat yourself. The moment you change your self-image is the moment people change their perception of you. However, you must understand that regardless of what anyone sees, says, or does, you need to see the best in you and give yourself the love you deserve and desire.

The words "God is love" made me realize if I say God is love and He lives within me that means I am love and what comes through me and starts with me is love. The love within will become evident and reflect in my appearance, attitude, and every area concerning my manner of living. You must know the love you choose not to give yourself can't be effectively given to others. Love is truly the most treasured gift, and others are aware of your ability to love them more than yourself (not so good in an equal relationship).

Think back to the last time you thought you were in love. There was absolutely nothing you wouldn't do for the other person. Nothing seemed to bother you; it was like sheer heaven on earth, because in your mind you were both in love and experiencing what love had to offer. But the moment the love you were giving didn't match up with your mindset, everything you were giving and thought you were receiving came to a complete halt. And then frustration set in: why weren't you experiencing the love you felt in the beginning?

Oftentimes the love you give will not be the love you receive, and when that occurs you become bitter and frustrated. The reason for this in many instances is because who you're seeking it from may not have the knowledge of what love is and what it does. And you now know the love you're seeking can only be found within.

There comes a time in life, love, and relationships when you must stop lavishing your treasures on others and start to lavish yourself with all the love and affection you desire. Just like many of us were before we started the process to wholeness, people are unaware of how to love because they haven't learned the art of loving themselves. This is why so many become selfish; they don't have an understanding of love, which is about action.

If you don't love yourself, how can someone else love, cherish, and respect you? This is why you want to lavish yourself with all good things and allow people to see how you love and treat yourself. That way they have no excuse for not treating you the way you deserve to be treated. When you raise the bar and love yourself, you'll adopt an attitude of gratitude and will no longer settle for less than what you're giving yourself.

In the process of loving ourselves, we must become determined, as it's easy to focus on others rather than ourselves. However, I can honestly say that what you don't give to yourself, you can't fully give to others, and when you give to others first before yourself, you'll feel depleted and empty. Additionally, what you don't give to yourself, you can't receive from others!

As a woman you must become sure in yourself and in your love, because an unsure mind will produce negative attitudes in yourself and others and will result in uncertain relationships. Take note of royal families and the lineage of Kings and Queens. When their children are born, they're automatically princes and princesses. Yet, although they're born into their royal title, they still must be groomed for that manner of living and be taught the duties and expectations befitting royalty.

In the same vein, although we all have the trait and capacity to love, we must be taught how to love. The key to loving is to treat others as you would treat yourself. For if you don't have self-love you won't be able to truly love others. Understand that love is an action word, and without supporting action, the words "I love you" are just empty words. Everyone won't be loved the same, but because love begins with you, the love others need will be evident and simpler to manifest.

Here are several traits or actions of love according to the great book I study, the Bible:

1. Love never gives up.

2. Love cares more for others than for self (but you can't care for others without first loving self)

3. Love doesn't want what it doesn't have

4. Love isn't boastful

5. Love isn't conceited

6. Love doesn't force itself on others

7. Love doesn't keep score on how many times someone has done wrong

8. Love doesn't take pleasure in the suffering of others

9. Love takes pleasure in the truth

10. Love puts up with everything

11. Love trusts God

12. Love always looks for the best and never the worst

13. Love never looks back but continues to move forward

The true test is to implement these love actions in your life so you can share them with others. Fulfillment and wholeness give evidence of these traits, and once you begin to love yourself, you're like a lighthouse in the middle of the ocean for everyone to see. You shine your light on every good quality you have within, and intrigue others to experience the same love which draws them closer to you.

Recipe

1) The 13 traits of love are the key to peace and serenity.

2) Love yourself in order to love others.

3) Don't allow past circumstances to dictate how and who you'll love based on fear and regret.

4) Understand that every word of "I love you" that others claim is true isn't truth unless you see supporting action that includes the 13 traits (from the Bible).

Exercise

It's time to implement the traits of love in your daily life to reach fulfillment. I've listed 13 traits which you'll explore through words and action. Over the next six weeks, practice these exercises that you can fit in your everyday actions.

Week 1

It's easy to quit when you're not seeing results and it seems a waste of time; however, if it's someone or something you love, don't give up. What is something you've wanted to do for some time, however you never got around to it? This week that's what I want you to do: whether it's starting a diet, writing in your journal, beginning a project... No matter what it is, love it and yourself enough to stick with it for one week. (DO NOT QUIT!)

Week 2

Have you ever noticed a spoiled child who's thrown a temper tantrum because they can't have what they want? Yet as soon as they get it, they walk around with an evil grin and a "na na na na na" attitude. Many of us are the same way: we want something we simply can't have and have made no effort to obtain other than pouting and hating others who have it. And even at the moment we obtain it, we have an attitude that's boastful, prideful, and full of conceit. This week choose not to reflect on what you don't have; be thankful for what you do have, that which you've been blessed with. If what you have is overflowing, this week choose not to have an attitude of conceit or the behavior of better than. If you have an over abundance of shoes in your closet, bless someone else with your extras. This is a way to show others love as well as yourself, and the result will be a feeling of peace.

Week 3

Be aware that love is not forceful, and you can't make someone feel about you what you may feel about them. This week will be a time of evaluating relationships—whether work related, family, marriage, or friendship. Have you ever been told that you always want your own way?. Do you always want your own way and try to force your opinions and ideas on others whether right or wrong? Discover how you may change that trait within. Take time to discover you this week, and what makes you act and react. Have a conversation with someone close to you, not as way of them telling you who you are, but as a simple survey into how they see you. The information obtained will allow a bit more insight on how you can become more attentive to your needs as well as those of others.

Week 4

Holding grudges is quite unproductive, because it causes bitterness and anger and allows no time for love as it focuses on the wrongs of others. Someone has hurt you, so you hold that grudge in order to see the person who wronged you hurt as well. This will be a week of forgiveness, regardless of what others have done to you or how many times it has been done. Remember your first priority is always you and living a fulfilled life, so why would you allow animosity or unforgiveness to make you wrinkled from the frowns in your face, or cause you to act out of character, or to remain in anger and unforgiveness so long that it affects your health. This week you're letting go and erasing the mental scoreboard you've kept against people who've hurt you. And even if they're experiencing their karma, don't revel in it with joy. (LET IT GO!)

Week 5

Regardless of popular belief, the best thing you can give to yourself and others is honesty. Why choose to live in a lie and not have the ability to keep up with the lie? Most people do this to "keep up with the Joneses." However, if they lived in the truth that their money or resources only extended so far, it would relieve slot of stress. So this week I encourage you to take pleasure in whatever your truth is. Know that the truth has the ability to set you free. Because it allows you the ability of living stress free and not having to make others believe that a lie is your reality. Live in the truth. Speak the truth. Allow truth to bring you pleasure through freedom.

Week 6

Stop expecting the worst in people and situations; everything is not always bad. Sometimes it's the choices we make that bring negativity, but even in those times do your best to see the good in it. Know that regardless of good or bad, it's a learning experience which will enable you to move forward and not make the same mistake again. Nothing that happens in your life is negative; it always has a positive aspect, but it's up to you to turn it around. Look for the best in whatever happens this week. Wake up with an attitude of gratitude, and determine to turn any negative into a positive.

NOTES

Money (Lack and Abundance)

"Money cures all ills" I've heard many say. I've also heard people say "Money is the root of all evil" which causes them to react certain ways to money. However, there's a misconception regarding money and what many think about the lack of or abundance of money. Understand that to have or want money is not evil; it's the love of money that can cause many to become wicked, conniving, or immoral in obtaining and keeping it.

There's a passage in the Bible that speaks of a rich, young ruler who wanted to share in the knowledge, wisdom, and presence of Christ. When he questioned how he could have this wisdom and knowledge, the reply he was given was that he must give up all his possessions and follow Christ. The young ruler at hearing this became saddened at the thought of giving up all his possessions. Why was he sad? It occurred to me that it was because this was what was known to him: his possessions were more important than wisdom, knowledge, and following Christ. He had put all his trust in the ability to obtain all he had through money.

The world we live in is obsessed with money and the idea of having plenty of it. If you look at the media or corporate America, so much weight has been placed on money that most people seem dissatisfied with their current income and will do anything to prove their financial status to impress or entice.

I determined years ago that no longer would I be a victim to the love of money and chase after it. It seemed like the more I chased, the further it ran from my existence. I chose to renew my mind and become a money magnet by being who I was created to be and allow money to chase me. Women especially fall victim to the love of money, because money creates status and gives us a sense of security. We must understand that the lack of or abundance of money doesn't determine our status and won't provide security if we're not wise.

Many are looking for others to care for them financially rather than relying on their own resources to create wealth for themselves. This is often why marriages and relationships are challenged and ultimately fail. Statistically for years it's been shown that money is the cause of over half the divorces, because someone is feeling like the other isn't pulling their weight financially. Truth be told, prior to entering the marriage, little to no conversation was had about how money would be handled.

I know many of you are wondering why I included this topic in a book about wholeness. Appreciate that the abundance of or lack of money doesn't determine your wholeness as others would lead you to believe. Because so much attention has been placed on money in our society, if you don't have a lot of wealth or status, you believe your life is not whole or full. Money is just an accessory to who you are and won't define your value.

The more you focus on attaining wealth as the path to fulfillment, the less you're able to see the other areas of your life that need attention or are already complete. And while your focus is on acquiring money, you'll either neglect the areas that need attention, or you'll focus on an area you feel money will solve. However, because your focus is more on money, you miss the need in hopes money will solve the problem. But due to your ambitious greed or neglect, the area of your life that needs a different resource than money ends up crumbling, because what you thought money would solve was not what was required for that situation.

Therefore, understand that the first sentence in this chapter is an untruth; money is not the cure for all ills. Certain areas in your life can't be fixed with money, and the quicker you understand that the more effective your process will become. So many of us spend our lives saving and planning for the future, which is a wise thing to do. However, if you're saving and planning in hopes that when trouble arises money will be the answer to the problem, it's possible that you're saving for what money won't be able to solve.

Often when women become emotional about an issue, they either turn to food or shopping as coping mechanisms, which is why the largest number of consumers is women. Because this resolution to the issue isn't generally effective, women have to work harder to maintain a certain lifestyle. That's why this process to wholeness is so important: not only will it enable women to know themselves better, it will also enable them to use more effective means of coping with life's challenges.

Can you imagine the countless dollars that could be saved by not spending emotionally? It isn't about the money loss, as we know money can be earned again with the right knowledge, but it's the underlying emptiness that causes an obsession with money that should concern us. People spend their entire lives chasing after money they don't have the ability to catch up with. And the frustration of not being able to attain the unattainable sets in when another receives what they were expecting to have.

The reason others have been able to obtain money without chasing it is many have learned and understood that when you align your life properly, what you want has no choice but to be attracted to you. Whether you have a lack of or an abundance of money, your focus should be on maintaining your peace, serenity, wisdom, and knowledge, which is what being whole is about. And as your mind is renewed, money becomes less of a priority, because your spirit is now open to receive true wealth—a value of wholeness which is priceless.

Recipe

1) Don't allow money to dictate your path or emotions.

2) Observe your intention or motive for obtaining wealth.

3) No longer chase what you can't catch.

Exercise

Allow your creativity to create money for you. Let it chase you! There's a scripture that says that your gifts will make room for and set you before great kings. *Use your gifts, talents, or skills and watch them work for you!*

Change your perception of money. The more you look at it as unattainable, the more it will continue to be unattainable to you.

NOTES

God
(Creator and Guide)

We all have our ideas about God. Some have chosen to make money, houses, cars, jobs, and even relationships their God. But not all have actually taken the time to see God in the beauty of His creation rather than the fleeting beauty of these material items.

I can recall driving down the street one day, looking at the greenery on the mountains and the blue sky, while breathing in the freshness of the air. I thought to myself how creative God is, knowing that everything He created began with a thought and a spoken word. Many just think of God as the creator of the universe and source of all moral authority, but He is so much more than that. He's the peace we need, the love we desire, and the provider we asked for. It's important to acknowledge that as creator of all, including you, everything He created carries a piece of Him.

Understand that you'll never discover who you are until you discover the one who created you. In my journey, love was the most desirable goal, and it wasn't until I made the decision to be close to my creator that I discovered true love. I discovered the one who created me was love, and because I'm a part of creation, love resides within me. However, I needed to align my thoughts and actions to that which is love.

So I learned all the attributes of that love (God) and began to receive the characteristics of that love. The more I became aware of the power within, the more it altered my understanding of who I was and who I was to become.

Many think those who have a belief in God are disconnected from reality; however, it's the exact opposite. Those who believe in God are aware of the empowerment that lies within and are determined to allow that authority to guide our lives—understanding that without allowing a higher authority to guide our lives, we'll be walking blindly through life. No matter how you get to that understanding—whether through meditation or prayer—know that without guidance you're susceptible to erroneous thinking.

In my life I've experienced losses in relationships and material possessions, and I've wondered what to do and how I could make changes to better my life and situation. Those were times I had to pray to seek answers and receive wisdom and knowledge. What I found was the more I sought wisdom, the more I needed to study the Bible—and the answers started to flow from within.

For me, God is the source I rely on for peace, strength, love, wisdom, and knowledge. Without Him I realize I can do nothing. This was most illuminated to me when I was homeless and lost everything. I had no other resources to turn to, which left me with no option but to trust that He had placed enough inside me to make the right decisions.

Some think that if they sit and do nothing, God will magically make things all right. However, when the Bible speaks of waiting on God, either prior to or following that statement, you must take action. Meaning in order to wait on God, you must put action behind it, which is where faith is put into action. What you believe will happen you also need to put action behind, like with your journey to self-worth.

Rest in the knowledge that God is everything we need, especially in a world that has lost hope. During my time of challenge and hardship, the knowledge of God kept me hopeful, and since everything I needed He had already placed inside me, all I had to do was tap into that power. The power within helped restore my hopes that life would get better for me and my family, and I would discover meaning and purpose for my life. I had hope that God would guide me through my journey so I could experience the true depth of His love.

When you discover on your journey renewed hope, the God kind of hope, nothing becomes impossible for you. That's the ultimate level of wholeness, where you see life not as it is but as it will be. The invisible becomes visible because of the knowledge of who God is in the process of becoming whole.

Many have stopped believing in God or choose not to believe because they've lost hope. At times everything may not work out as planned or hoped for, and we often look for someone or something to blame. And what tends to happen when there's a belief in God is He gets blamed for what's not happening. But I can share with you that it's not God alone who produces results in your life. God isn't a genie as many would like to portray Him. God is a sovereign being, there to assist, guide, and provide instructions for the path of your life.

Although paths vary, the destination of completeness in every area of life is the same destination for all, no matter when, how, or where we arrive. Just rest assured that your wholeness is a part of God's plan and desire for your life. Because as you become whole, you have the ability to share with others how to walk the same path of wholeness.

Recipe

1) Discover the Higher Power within.

2) Be confident that the small voice you hear is guiding your life in the right direction.

3) Believe that God is everything you need Him to be and has placed what you need inside.

4) Then put into action what you believe.

Exercise

Pray. Many times we find all the words to say when we talk to friends, family, and clergy in hopes that they can help us solve an issue or give us the option to vent. We don't know if these people are trustworthy and will keep the confidence of what we've shared. Yet I've found with God, I'm able to say everything I feel and ask for what I need. Whether others believe it or not, because I believe I'll have results, I've received them. And it was all kept in confidence, never to be heard by anyone but God. Take time to pray and speak what you would to a trusted friend and even what you can't tell anyone—except God!

NOTES

Readiness
(To Begin Your Journey)

Various areas of life play a part in your journey to fulfillment, some of which I've included in this book to help you on your path. I find that women are multifaceted which allows them to be everything to everybody at any time. However, the challenge for them has been choosing to be everything for themselves at the times they need to.

Over the years of speaking with women, I've seen them struggle to learn their true nature, because they often get lost in their titles and duties rather than the truth of who they are. They've lost their identity and have no clue how to get it back. This is what causes the emptiness, lack of fulfillment, and feeling of not being whole. So many women have yet to discover who they are, and instead of taking the time out to find out, they find their identity outside themselves, whether in a friend, boyfriend, husband, job, or kids.

It took me a while to discover myself, because I allowed others to define who I was through my titles or roles. Know that in searching for or discovering your identity, you might find it a rather painful experience. A few souls may mistake you attempting to be you as being offensive to them as you move into being who you've not been. They're used to you being and acting a certain way. You have to be willing to lose some people, even family, because they think they're helping you by telling you to be who they want you to be.

Expect to be misunderstood, because when you don't know who you are, other people want to chime in with negativity as they're unsure of themselves. Be prepared to make the ultimate sacrifice. Your sacrifice may vary, but in my case it involved friendships and intimate relationships. Regardless of the cost of that sacrifice, it's a necessary decision for your self-worth that will produce more than what you thought you lost. When you've attained wholeness and know who you are, a boldness comes upon you, and when you know who you are and stand in your completeness fear, doubt, and disbelief are diminished.

Now that you've read this book and have arrived at Readiness, it's time to ask yourself these important questions: Who am I as a woman? Am I ready to be whole in every area of my life? Am I committed to my journey?

I previously said that the act of sharing Wedding Cake comes at the end of the wedding event, but in wholeness the Wedding Cake recipe is just the beginning of your journey. Getting to fulfillment requires daily practice and determination. It's not a quick fix to a changed life; however, this book is intended to be a guide to help you along the way, to help you better understand you, and to know that you can implement the changes necessary to upgrade your manner of living.

I ask you to understand that you're the only one who can make your Wedding Cake (wholeness) by using the ingredients and recipes you'll be given through meditation and focus. These tools will show you how to meditate on your desires, dreams, and aspirations in order to demolish thoughts of negativity—as well as bring your mind back to serenity and peace by relaxing and not being overly concerned about what you can't control or change.

You must recognize that the only control you have is over yourself, which allows you to change your manner of living into what's best for you and creates an environment for success. We're all unique, and although we may go about success in different ways, the formula is the same. No matter what step you're on, take the time to revel in the beauty that's you, flawed and all. Know that even with flaws, you're beautifully and wonderfully created, and you must take pleasure in everything that is you.

In your readiness for your journey to fulfillment, be aware of how powerful your words and thoughts are. Be conscious of what you speak, as your words will manifest in the context they're sent into the universe. Many may not believe this concept, however in my conversations with women, they often ask, "Why do more bad things happen to me than good?" My reply is always, "Your words are powerful and ultimately are birthed from your thoughts. What you think is what you expect, and your expectation is what you receive." It's not a reason for guilt or blame, just self responsibility.

If every situation you've had in your life has been bad or negative, it's because that's what you expected to receive. How can you expect to receive anything good if your thoughts and words are negative? Good may not be what you're accustomed to receiving so you don't ask for or receive it. The more you speak, the more you believe, and your belief turns into expectation, and the result of expectation is the product of your words. This is why your readiness depends on the words, thoughts, beliefs, and expectations of your success! When we hear the word "success" we may equate it to various areas including money and career, but success should be attained in every area of your life.

I'm sure that through this journey to wholeness you'll attain great success and will continue to learn a lot about yourself. Meditation will bring the understanding of your thoughts into perspective and allow you to see where your mind is at concerning yourself and those around you. You need to be focused to quiet the noise of your environment and create peace, which brings clarity and sets the foundation for change. That foundation includes your character, your attitude, love, and caring for others, especially yourself. And remember, your beauty is the combination of your outer appearance and inner being, which illuminates your self-worth. This is why you're able to love and treat others as you would yourself, because of the value you've now placed on your worth. The love you're able to give is the love you have for yourself.

My hopes and prayers are that this book leads you on your path to wholeness with the understanding that at some point or another you must discover who you are, and without this journey success is merely a thought, a wish, and a dream. You've now readied yourself to receive more instructions for your journey as you've allowed this guide to open your mind and heart to change.

Understand this process is one that many can't undertake as they're afraid to be introduced to themselves. They're comfortable in the fantasy they've created in their mind of who they are and what their lives should be. However, no one can be you, and you can't be anyone else no matter how you try to make changes. It's like having two puzzles and trying to swap pieces to make the other picture complete. No matter how much you work at it, something will always look out of place.

When your cake is ready, you have to take out the oven and let it cool. But just because it came out of the oven, that's not the end of the process. You now have to decorate it. This is how the Wedding Cake is different from any other cake: you can now add all the bells, whistles, bows, and toppers, to make it look exquisite. The inner is ready, and now you can dress up the outer, which makes for a more edible and presentable cake.

Take the time to enjoy what this process brings, and watch as others notice the new you that's comparable to both outer and inner beauty. I'm here any time you need support on your journey to fulfillment.

Exercise

Enjoy the recipe to wholeness. It's now time to celebrate and eat cake!

NOTES

About the Author

Ann K Ross has dedicated her life to empowering women to regain their strength and identity with their own personal inner power. She has participated as leader to many youth and women's organizations, which has led to her title as mentor, personal advisor, life coach, and minister.

Ann has built her career in customer service, where she learned to listen to the needs of people and provide solutions. This has allowed her over the years to listen to the concerns of women and to motivate them through life's experiences to produce change. She lives by the knowledge that everyone can transform or change their lives with dedication and focus.

Born in 1976 in an era of change, Ann is a native of Compton, California and has lived in Los Angeles County throughout her life. She has worked as producer for a popular radio show, and is an author and motivational speaker. But most importantly she's a mother of two daughters.

www.ingramcontent.com/pod-product-compliance
Lightning Source LLC
LaVergne TN
LVHW051104080426
835508LV00019B/2059